“He who is not courageous enough to take risks will accomplish nothing in life

MUHAMMAD ALI – THE GREATEST

Feats of Clay

A mutual love affair between Cassius Clay and the British people began as he arrived for his fight with Henry Cooper

IN MAY 1963, The Beatles' fame was growing as their music captured the attention of Britain and led a cultural revolution that spread worldwide.

That same month, another big noise arrived from across the Atlantic.

Cassius Clay, then 21 and unbeaten in 18 fights, flew into London ahead of his first fight outside the USA. His opponent was the beloved local hero, Henry Cooper.

As soon as he landed, Clay went into overdrive, capturing attention and imagination with his style, sense of humour and outrageous boasting. We had never seen or heard anything like it.

An unfamiliar city did not dent his supreme self-confidence, as he proclaimed: "I'm not the greatest. I'm the double greatest. Not only do I knock 'em out, I pick the round. I'm the boldest, the prettiest, the most superior, most scientific, most skilfullest fighter in the ring today. I'm the onliest fighter who goes from corner to corner and club to club debating with fans. I've received more publicity than any fighter in history. I talk to reporters till their fingers are sore."

HELLO LONDON: A wave and a round prediction as he lands on Britain soil for the first time, May 1963

THE BODYGUARD: Ronald King keeps watch while Clay sleeps in his Piccadilly hotel room

FEATS OF CLAY

May 28 1963

CASSIUS ARRIVES

12

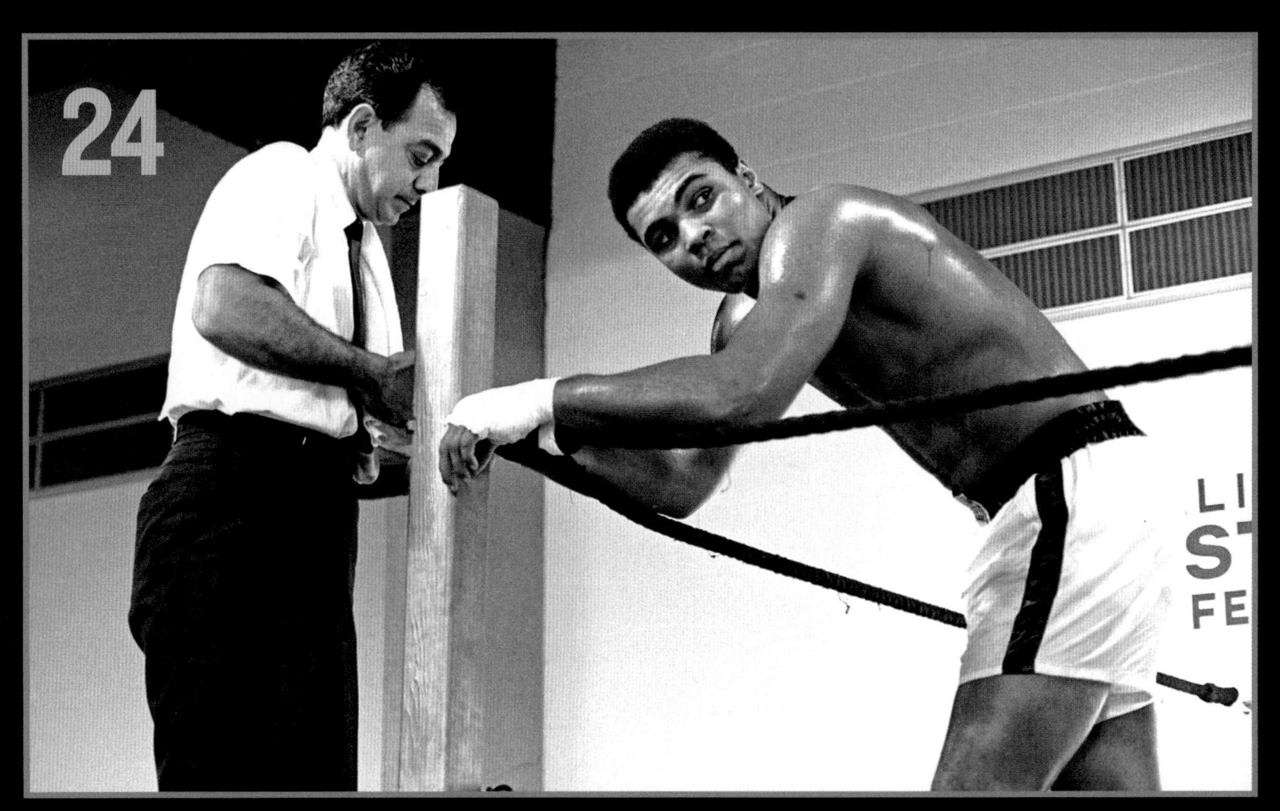

62

The last hurrah before the FINAL BELL

After being outpointed by Leon Spinks, Ali avenged the loss to become the first three-time world heavyweight champion before his career closed with two [illegible]

IN FEBRUARY 1978, Muhammad Ali had just turned 36 when he defended his title against the novice Leon Spinks – a 1976 Olympic gold medallist, but only seven fights into his professional career

A complacent, demotivated, out of shape Ali was outpointed by Spinks in one of the biggest upsets in boxing history.

Seven months later there was a rematch in New Orleans. This time Ali was fully prepared and he won a comfortable decision over 15 rounds, which meant he was the first man to win the heavyweight title three times.

There didn't appear to be anything left for Ali to achieve and after a few months of reflection, the man himself appeared to agree, announcing his retirement in June 1979.

Sadly, like so many boxers, he couldn't resist a comeback, agreeing to fight the unbeaten champion Larry Holmes in October 1980.

The health problems that would blight his later life were making themselves evident and Ali was a mirage of the thrilling fighter of old. Now he was just old. Trainer Angelo Dundee called a halt to the slaughter after ten depressing rounds.

There was one final fight – a points loss to Trevor Berbick in the Bahamas in December 1981 – before, belatedly, Ali retired for good.

63

CONTENTS

Mirrorcollection

HEAD OF SYNDICATION & LICENSING: FERGUS MCKENNA
MIRRORPIX: mirrorpix.com 020 7293 3700

PRODUCED BY TRINITY MIRROR MEDIA, PO BOX 48, LIVERPOOL, L69 3EB

MANAGING DIRECTOR: STEVE HANRAHAN
COMMERCIAL DIRECTOR: WILL BEEDLES
EXECUTIVE EDITOR: PAUL DOVE
EXECUTIVE ART EDITOR: RICK COOKE
DESIGN & PRODUCTION: LEE ASHUN
COMPILED AND WRITTEN BY: ALAN JEWELL

PRINTED BY: WILLIAM GIBBONS

Part of the Mirror Collection

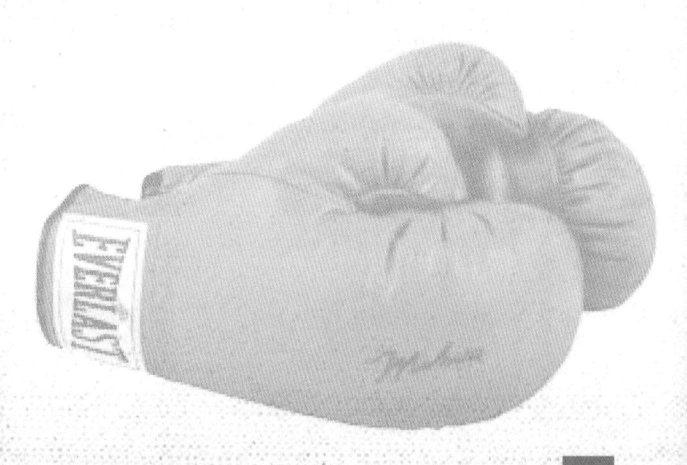

THE ONE AND ONLY

Nobody entertained us, thrilled us, moved us like Muhammad Ali. He leaves behind cherished memories and an incredible legacy

The great American novelist, Norman Mailer, identified Muhammad Ali as 'the very spirit of the 20th century'. His passing in the 21st gives us all time to reflect, mourn but, above all, celebrate a man who enriched our lives in so many ways for so long.

Ali coined his own epitaph: He was, quite simply, The Greatest.

No one from any era, any sphere, was as recognisable, as popular, as loved. His fame had no boundaries. All countries and all ages knew about Muhammad Ali.

We were entranced by his charisma, intelligence, humour and bravery. That handsome face, lightning wit and ready charm cast an irresistible spell. He possessed an intoxicating presence.

Pop singers, movie stars and, these days, reality television creations can have teenagers scrambling to get near them but not many people have the same effect on middle-aged men or elderly ladies.

Born as Cassius Marcellus Clay, the grandson of a slave, into the segregationist city of Louisville, Kentucky, in January 1942, he wasn't going to allow himself to be categorised in any way. He was unique, a total one-off.

Young Cassius's path into our lives was set when his new $60 bicycle was stolen in 1954. Aged 12 and

nursing a burning sense of injustice, he sought out a local white policeman, Joe Martin, and urged the officer to find the thief so Cassius could "whup him". Martin persuaded him to channel his anger and energy into a neighbourhood boxing class he ran. Whoever could have known?

Within six years Clay was winning Olympic gold in the light-heavyweight class at the Rome Olympics. Months later his professional career began. It wouldn't be long before we began to hear about it, with the chief cheerleader being the man himself.

The combination of his unorthodox boxing talent and extrovert, occasionally outrageous personality demanded attention. It was his luck – and ours – that his burgeoning career flowered as a revolution in communications technology ushered in the media age. Television was taking hold, allowing us to see and hear about people and events on the other side of the world. His second fight with Sonny Liston, in 1965, was the first sporting event in America to be televised live in Britain via satellite.

That wasn't the first time we'd seen him, though. In 1963, Clay, unbeaten in 18 fights, came to Britain to fight the home hope, Henry Cooper. Even as he was walking down the aeroplane's steps at Heathrow, he was boasting to waiting cameras about what round (the fifth) in which he would finish Cooper off. People flocked around him from the start, drawn by his open nature. Many were amused by his brash statements, many were not, but everyone had an opinion about the American visitor and nobody could ignore him.

Although Cooper famously dumped the young upstart on his backside, Clay got up to do as he said by stopping Henry in round five. Less than 12 months later he fulfilled another prediction by humiliating the formidable, frightening Liston and claiming the World Heavyweight Championship. It was then, unquestionably, the greatest prize in sport and he had won it, barely 22 years old. He was a physical marvel.

Within days he formally embraced the militant Nation of Islam, which argued for the separation of the races and regarded white people as "devils", and changed his name to Muhammad Ali. This served to alienate him further from an American audience that was already quite hostile to the new champion.

Those resistant to his charms felt he was unpatriotic, 'un-American' even, and this feeling would only deepen when he refused to be drafted into the armed services during the Vietnam War, having famously declared: "I ain't got no quarrel with them Vietcong."

As the matter came to a head, Ali fought on and kept winning with some stunning performances. Cleveland Williams was taken apart in 1966. In three rounds Ali landed over 100 punches, his hapless challenger just three. No boxer could

FROM LEFT TO RIGHT:

***PRECOCIOUS:* Cassius Clay, aged 12, shortly after taking up boxing**

***FRESH-FACED:* Taping his hands before a sparring session**

***FIRST MEETING:* Aged 20, he chats to a five-year-old girl called Lonnie, who lived opposite his mother's house in Louisville. Ali and Lonnie married in 1986**

live with him. His style – described by the famed boxing writer, AJ Liebling, as 'skittering... like a pebble over water' – was too fast for his opponents.

The one adversary he couldn't overcome was the American government. Still unbeaten, and just 25, he was stripped of his title in 1967, prosecuted for the 'crime' of refusing the draft and condemned to exile in his own land after having his passport revoked. He ruefully remarked: "Man, boxing is child's play compared with this fight."

> **"Robbed of his prime years, we never got to see the best of Ali, the boxer"**

As he wasn't allowed a licence to box, he gave speeches in universities, lecturing on social, political and religious issues. As time passed, opinion about the war began to shift. Opposition grew and many people came round to understanding Ali's point of view.

For all his verbosity, boxing remained his primary means of self-expression and he was able to return to the ring in late 1970. However, the dazzling leg speed that allowed him to elude opponents' attacks had diminished. In retrospect, robbed of his prime years, we realise that we never saw the best of Ali, the boxer. From now on, he would have to call on the deep reservoir of his cunning and courage as he fought younger, stronger, fearsome men.

Joe Frazier, who was now the heavyweight champion, handed Ali his first defeat in the 'Fight of the Century' in March 1971. They would meet in the ring twice more and they defined each other's careers. Frazier asked more questions of Ali than any other fighter.

However, the peak of his career came when he knocked out George Foreman in the 'Rumble in the Jungle' in 1974 to reclaim the heavyweight title seven-and-a-half years after it was taken from him. Before the fight, in Zaire (now DR Congo), Africa, he led the chants of "Ali, bomaye" (Ali, kill him) among besotted locals, but plenty of impartial observers felt it was Ali in mortal danger. Foreman had savagely cut down Frazier and Ken Norton, who had both beaten Ali. There were genuine fears that the champion was going to inflict a serious beating on the older man. Ali's victory stunned a world he ruled once more. Yet again, he turned fantasy into fact.

He reigned until 1978 when he lost to Leon Spinks before winning a rematch in September of that year, which made him world heavyweight champion for an unprecedented third time. By now a beloved figure, he retired after that fight but, inevitably, perhaps tragically, he came back, aged 38, to challenge Larry Holmes in October 1980. By then symptoms of the health problems that would blight his later life were apparent, but he was still allowed to get in the ring. Holmes battered Ali into submission after 11 one-sided rounds. Just over a year later there was one more pitiful fight, a loss to Trevor Berbick, before a final retirement.

After his boxing career ended, Ali effectively became an international missionary for peace, understanding and equality, maintaining a hectic travelling schedule that made few concessions to the ravages wrought by Parkinson's disease. As time passed, the booming voice was reduced to a husky whisper, he walked with an awkward shuffle and his arm shook uncontrollably, but Ali sought no sympathy. The illness was accepted with dignity and grace. There may have been personal frustration but he never betrayed any bitterness, seeing it all as part of God's plan for him.

In the foreword to an authorised 1996 book about himself, Ali wrote: 'I now believe that the life we lead on earth is but a mosquito's wing compared to eternity and life in the hereafter. And I've learned that whatever time we spend on earth should be spent helping others and creating justice and equality for all people.'

It may have been uncomfortable to witness him dealing with his ailments when lighting the Olympic flame in 1996, or receiving the BBC Sports Personality of the Century award three years later, but Ali was happy and didn't want to hide away. He always loved being around people, children especially, and the effect he had on others – the joy and love he inspired – never diminished.

We can't pretend he was perfect. Much of the Nation of Islam rhetoric he spouted in the 1960s and '70s went beyond the pale, and some of the insults aimed at Joe Frazier were offensive and unnecessary. He wasn't averse to playing the field either, while marrying four times and fathering nine children (seven daughters and two sons, one of whom was adopted). However, as he grew older, he grew wiser, embracing orthodox Islam and finding contentment in a loving marriage to Lonnie, his constant companion from 1986.

CENTRE OF ATTENTION:
Gleason's gym, New York, 1976

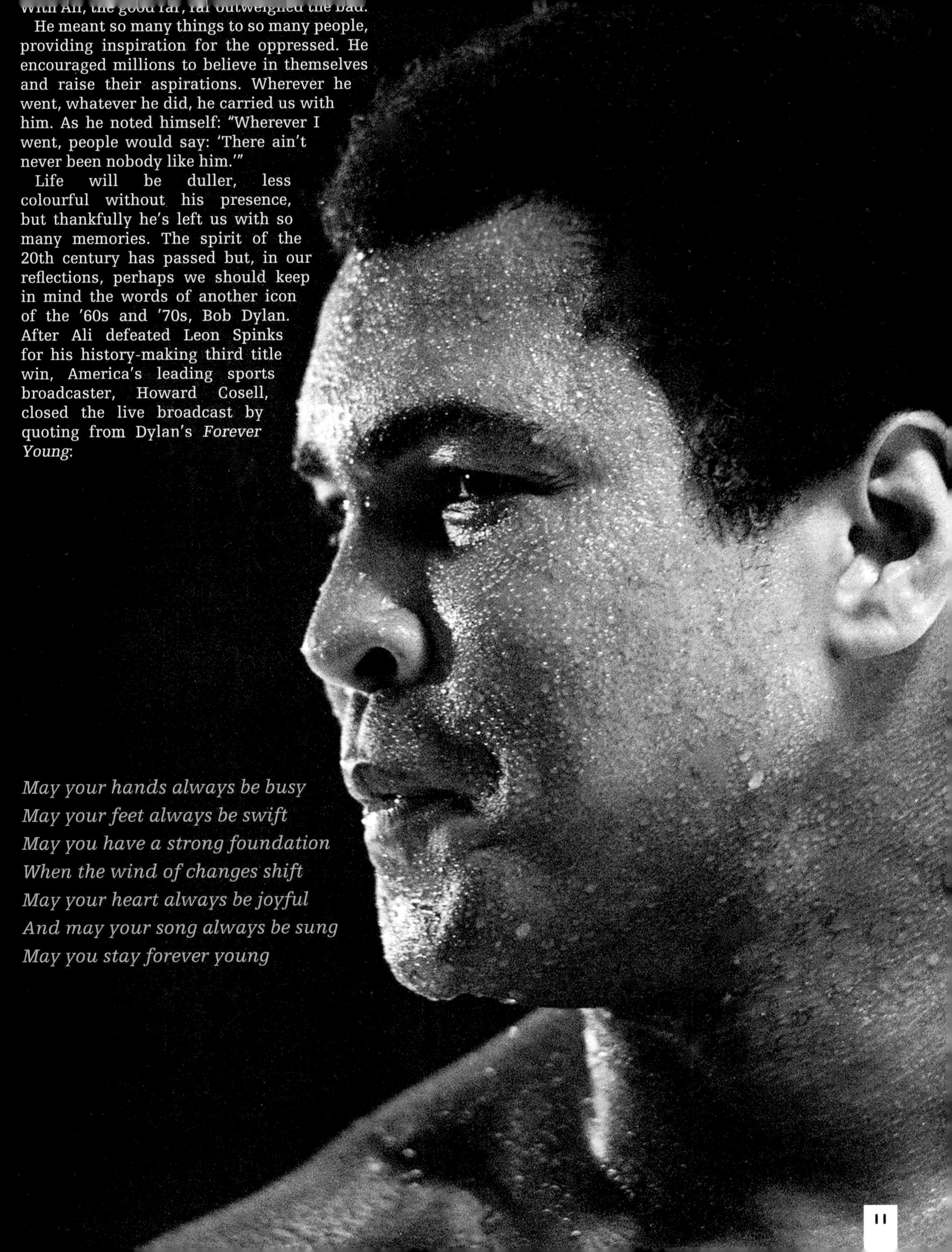

With Ali, the good far, far outweighed the bad.

He meant so many things to so many people, providing inspiration for the oppressed. He encouraged millions to believe in themselves and raise their aspirations. Wherever he went, whatever he did, he carried us with him. As he noted himself: "Wherever I went, people would say: 'There ain't never been nobody like him.'"

Life will be duller, less colourful without his presence, but thankfully he's left us with so many memories. The spirit of the 20th century has passed but, in our reflections, perhaps we should keep in mind the words of another icon of the '60s and '70s, Bob Dylan. After Ali defeated Leon Spinks for his history-making third title win, America's leading sports broadcaster, Howard Cosell, closed the live broadcast by quoting from Dylan's *Forever Young*:

May your hands always be busy
May your feet always be swift
May you have a strong foundation
When the wind of changes shift
May your heart always be joyful
And may your song always be sung
May you stay forever young

Feats of Clay

A mutual love affair between Cassius Clay and the British people began as he arrived for his fight with Henry Cooper

IN MAY 1963, The Beatles' fame was growing as their music captured the attention of Britain and led a cultural revolution that spread worldwide.

That same month, another big noise arrived from across the Atlantic.

Cassius Clay, then 21 and unbeaten in 18 fights, flew into London ahead of his first fight outside the USA. His opponent was the beloved local hero, Henry Cooper.

As soon as he landed, Clay went into overdrive, capturing attention and imagination with his style, sense of humour and outrageous boasting. We had never seen or heard anything like it.

An unfamiliar city did not dent his supreme self-confidence, as he proclaimed: "I'm not the greatest. I'm the double greatest. Not only do I knock 'em out, I pick the round. I'm the boldest, the prettiest, the most superior, most scientific, most skilfullest fighter in the ring today. I'm the onliest fighter who goes from corner to corner and club to club debating with fans. I've received more publicity than any fighter in history. I talk to reporters till their fingers are sore."

HELLO LONDON: A wave and a round prediction as he lands on British soil for the first time, May 1963

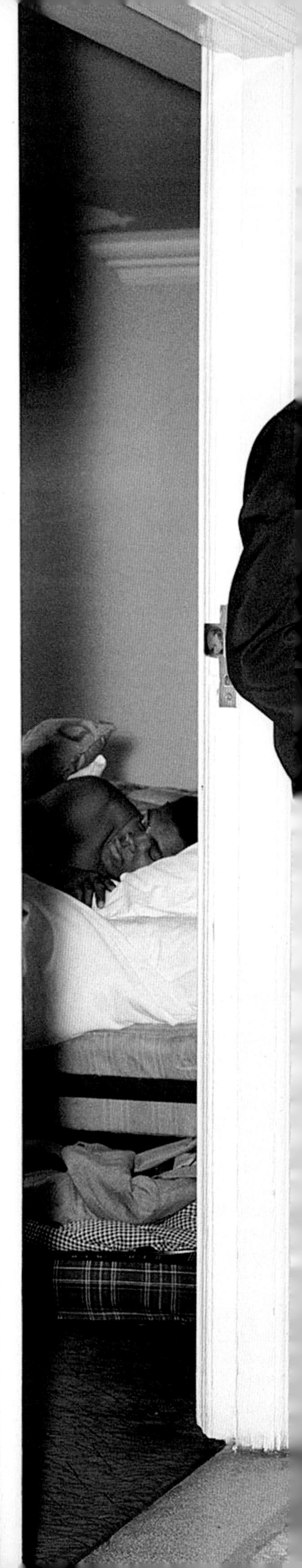

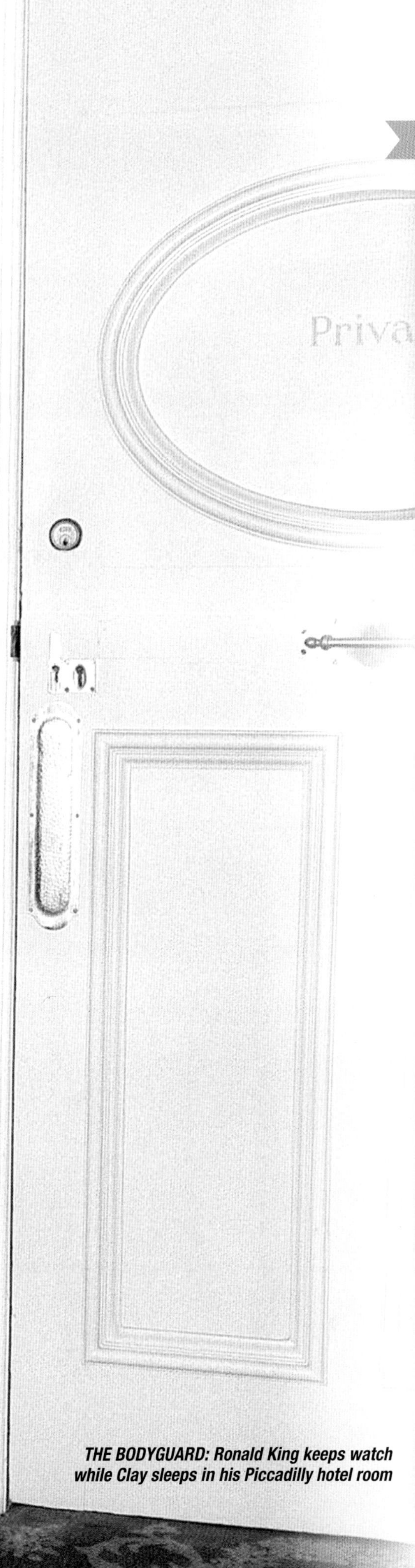

THE BODYGUARD: Ronald King keeps watch while Clay sleeps in his Piccadilly hotel room

May 28 1963

CASSIUS ARRIVES

By Peter Wilson

There has never been anything quite like it. He came, he saw and he talked.

He talked to television men. He talked to radio sound men. He talked to photographers. He talked to sports writers. He talked to promoters. Oh blimey! How he talked!

Who is he? Who else but Cassius Marcellus Clay, on whose own authority I have it that he is not only the greatest heavyweight in the world but the greatest the world has ever seen or is ever likely to see.

Nothing is too outrageous for Cassius Marcellus to blurt out. At lunch, with his opponent for June 18 at Wembley, Henry Cooper, sitting only two seats away, he said to me in a foghorn whisper: "Why did you allow this nice kid to fight me?" At 29, Cooper is nearly eight years older than Clay.

Between mouthfuls, someone mentioned Sonny Liston, who happens to be the world champion, but only, according to Clay, because he got there before Cassius Marcellus had his chance.

"Liston? That ugly great bear? I'm just filling in time until I annihilate him as well. But soon or late he'll fall in eight. He's too ugly to be a fighter. Real fighters are pretty like me."

MC Bud Flanagan referred to Cassius as "the greatest, most colourful fighter ever to come to England". It was too much for 'The Lip'. "Or anywhere else," he interrupted.

Despite the fact that he flew the Atlantic overnight, he never gave up talking.

THE MIRROR MAN: Chief sports writer Peter Wilson gets his ear chewed off

A CUT ABOVE: Getting a trim in the hairdressing salon of Austin Reed, with boxing promoter Jack Solomons in the chair next to him

HURDLER: Showing off his dexterity during a training run

CENTRE OF ATTENTION: Looking dapper as he strolls through central London, catching the eye of curious onlookers

HOLDING COURT: In full flow as BBC reporter Richard Woods attempts to get a word in

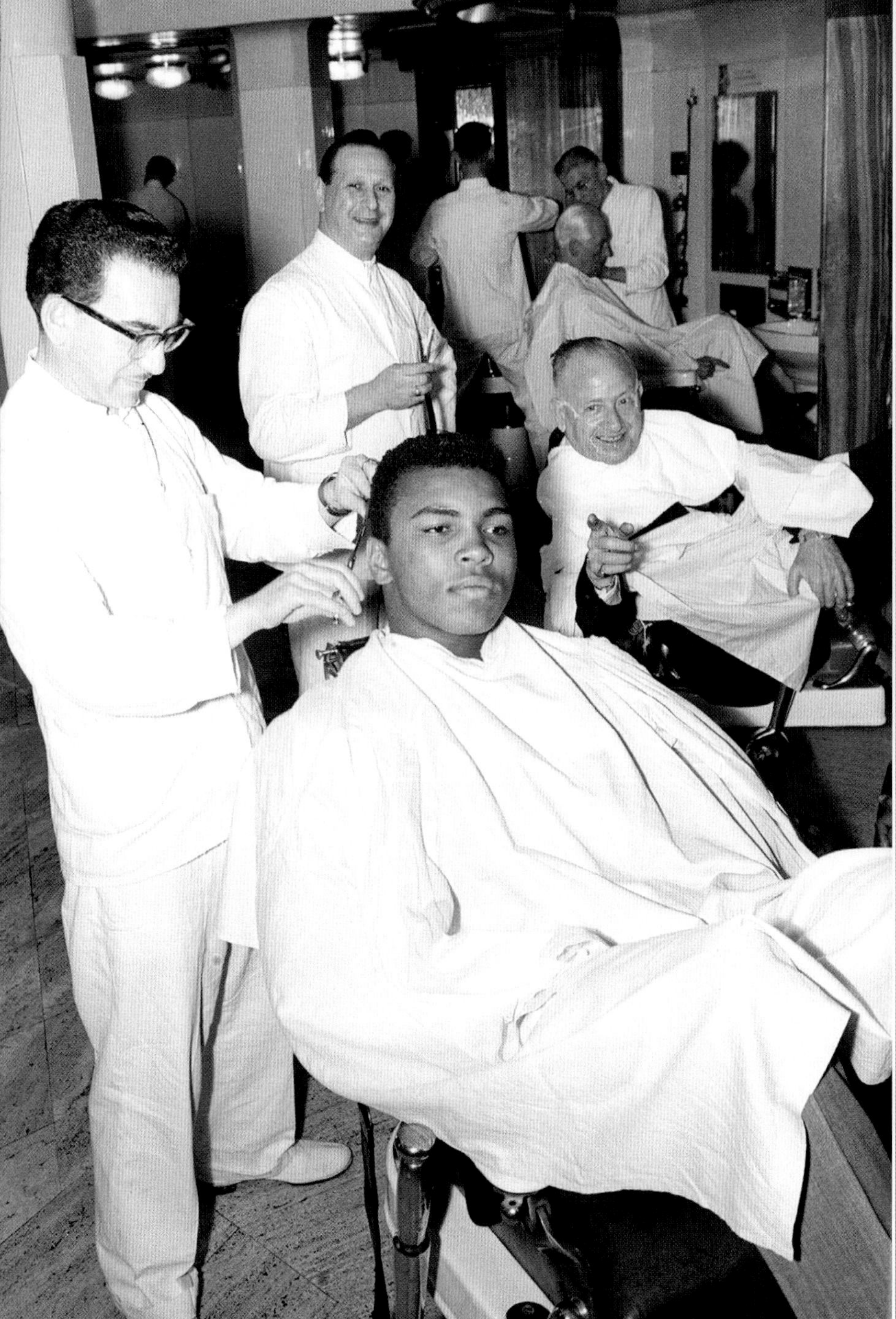

GREAT SCOT: Donning a kilt and Glengarry hat for an unusual photo opportunity before the Cooper fight

A DOUBLE
DIAMOND
works wonders
Have a Coke

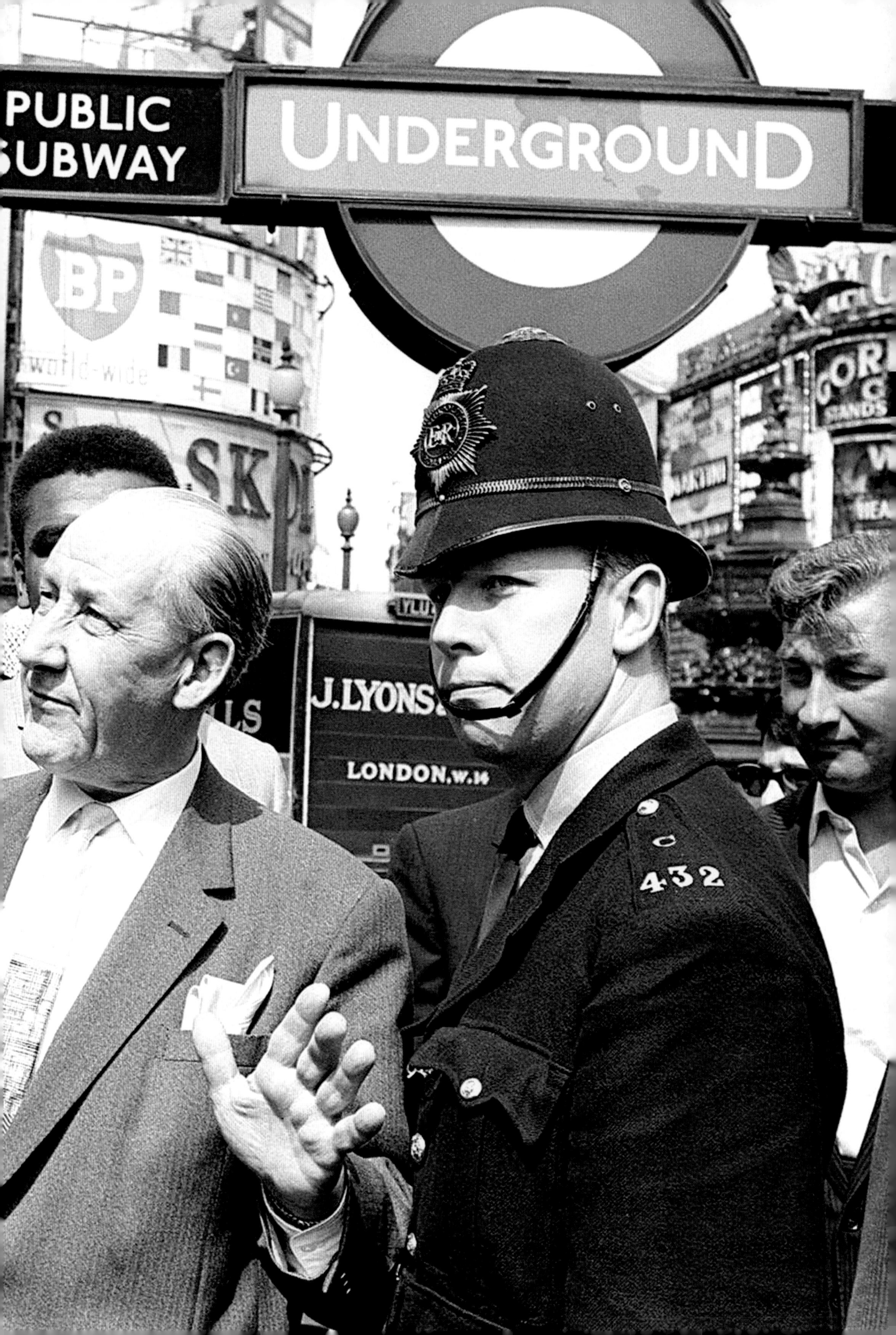

PUBLIC SUBWAY
UNDERGROUND
J. LYONS
LONDON. W.14
432

FOOD FOR THOUGHT: *Getting stuck into a steak at a restaurant in Brewer Street, Soho*

PLAY FIGHT: *Having some fun with six-year-old Patrick Power during a break in training*

WORKING UP A SWEAT: *Showing the effects of his exertions as he hones his condition ahead of the Cooper fight*

SCALES: During the weigh-in at the Odeon Theatre, Leicester Square. The wording on his gown shows he already considered himself 'The Greatest'

HIGH FIVE: Clay makes it clear the round in which he expects to stop Cooper as he drums up publicity at a British middleweight title fight. He said: "I won't stop running till every seat is sold"

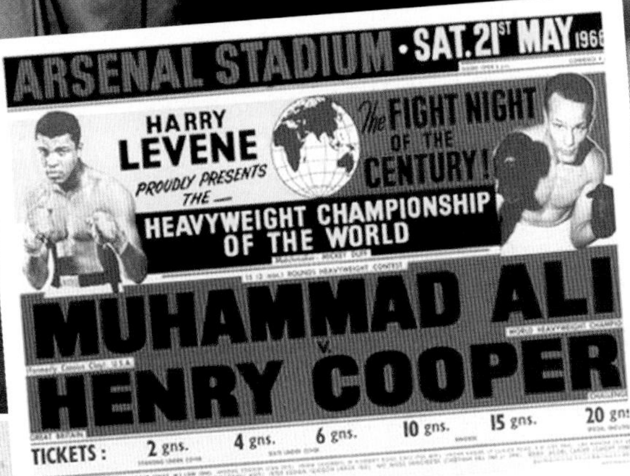

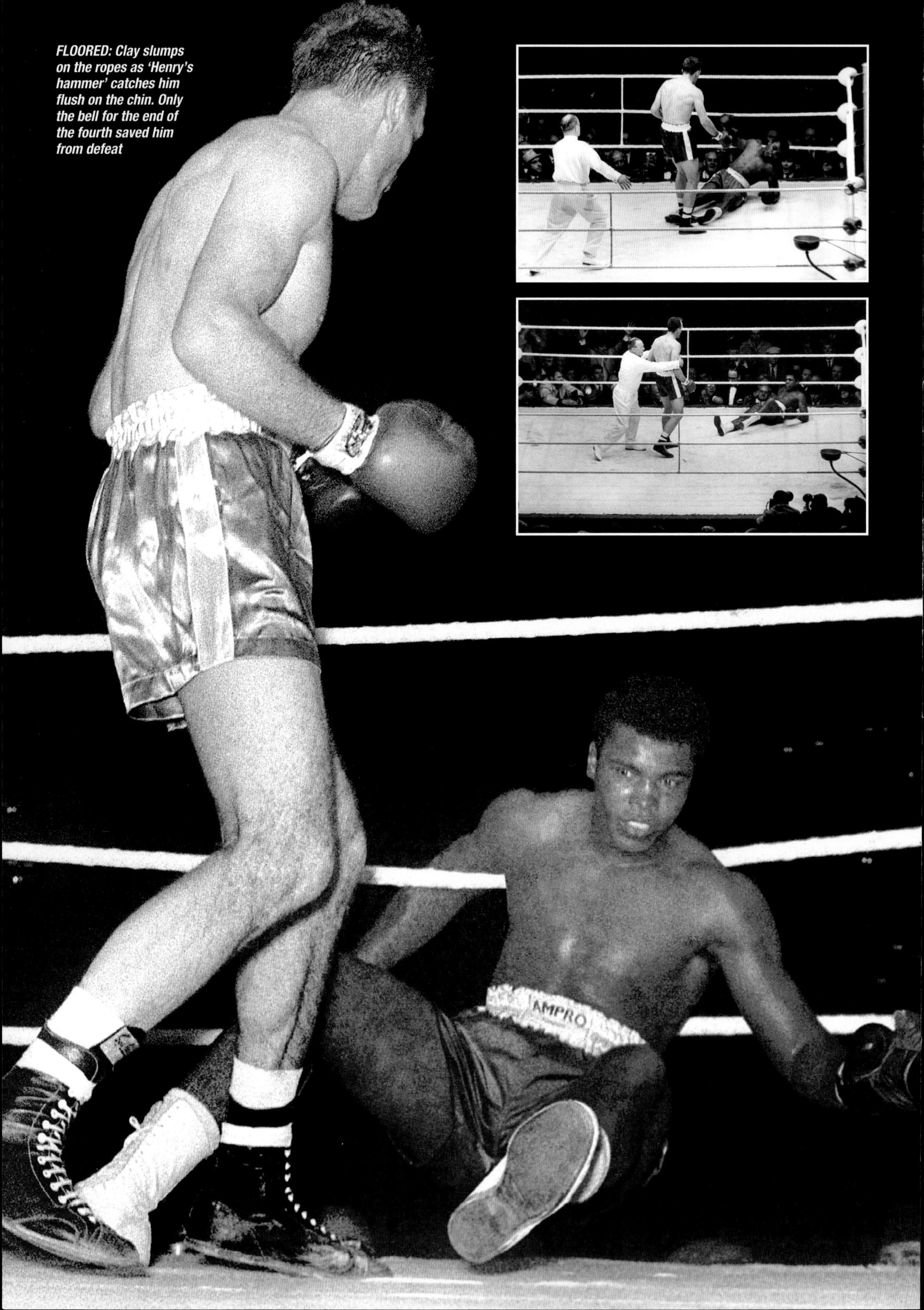

FLOORED: Clay slumps on the ropes as 'Henry's hammer' catches him flush on the chin. Only the bell for the end of the fourth saved him from defeat

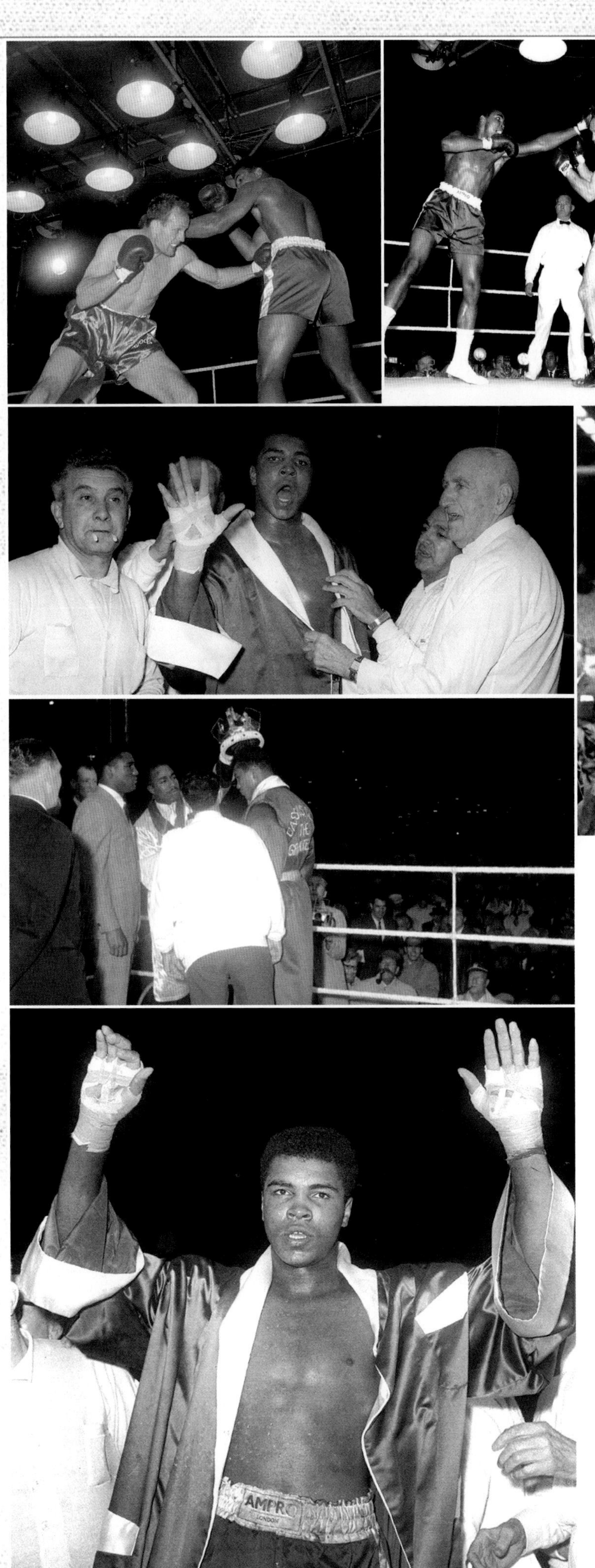

A NARROW ESCAPE

WEMBLEY Stadium was at fever pitch for the fight, with the patriotic crowd roaring their beloved Henry on against the brash braggart from America.

Clay fulfilled his prediction of stopping Cooper in the fifth but only after he was given the biggest fright of his nascent career. Cassius dominated the early exchanges and his dazzling flurries soon bruised and broke Cooper's fragile skin, causing significant cuts. Blood flowed down the left side of his face, obscuring his vision.

However, in the final seconds of the fourth Cooper exploded his famed left hook onto Clay's chin, lifting him off his feat and dumping him, dazed and confused, into the ropes.

In the excitement, most people didn't realise the bell had rung. Clay's trainer, Angelo Dundee, took advantage of the break between rounds to stretch further a split in the seam of his man's glove, delaying the resumption and allowing Clay's head to clear.

Once the fifth commenced, Clay tore into Cooper, battering him and deepening the wounds. A little over two minutes later, referee Tommy Little had no option but to stop the fight.

KEEPING CASSIUS COMPANY: A group of young ladies flock to Clay as he relaxes after the fight at the Piccadilly Hotel

CASSIUS CALLS FOR THE GIRLS

ON RETURNING to his hotel the night he beat Henry Coopewwr, Cassius Clay was welcomed by a "reception committee" of seven giggling girls, according to the following day's Daily Mirror.

Clay called: "Bring the queens over here."

Then he posed for pictures with the girls, with Mirror photographer Freddie Cole on hand to provide Cassius with an early edition of the paper so he could read about his own performance.

Wearing a dinner jacket and sipping iced lemonade, he held up his five fingers as he lounged on a settee.

Then he recited another poem: "The people thought I was talking jive, but I was right – I stopped Cooper in five."

'NEXT PREMIER' MOVES BEGIN

THE PROFUMOS COME HOME

'My profound remorse'

ARMY SCHOOL HIT BY TYPHOID

CLAY WINS IN FIVE WITH A 'BARE' FIST

READ ALL ABOUT IT: What did he make of Peter Wilson's report in the Daily Mirror?

DAILY MIRROR, Thursday, February 27, 1964

CASSIUS STRIKES—NOW THE INQUEST

State calls for medical reports on Liston

FOUR pictures tell the story of Cassius Clay's surprise defeat of Sonny Liston in their world heavyweight fight in Miami. But last night the inquest on the fight began.

The first move was made by the Florida State Attorney, Mr. Richard Gerstein.

He ordered the Miami Beach Boxing Commission to turn over all records and medical papers relating to Liston.

Puzzle

His retirement before the seventh round has puzzled US boxing critics.

Tired

The jubilant Cassius crows

THE EYE It's Round Three—one more than Liston envisaged. The blood is already spilling from a cut beneath his left eye as a punch from Clay rams into the other eye.

THE BLOW Still Round Three—and it's the punch that might have ended the whole affair. Home it goes to Liston's left shoulder, the shoulder that caused him to retire.

THE JOY For Cassius it's the moment of truth and of joy. Victory is his, as he promised it would be. The bell has gone for the seventh round. But Liston doesn't answer.

THE WOE His crown gone, the saddened Liston displays the left shoulder that stopped him defending himself. And a doctor's hand is seen, indicating the area of torn muscle.

CHAMPION OF THE WORLD

IN MAY 1964, Clay, as he put it himself, "shook up the world" when he forced the fearsome Sonny Liston to quit at the end of the sixth round of their heavyweight championship fight in Miami.

He had been a massive underdog and, to a man, the leading sports writers of Fleet Street had dismissed his chances (Liston was 7/1 on). On February 27, the front page of the Daily Mirror carried pictures of the boxing experts – including the Mirror's own Peter Wilson – and declared them 'The Men with Red Faces'.

Clay appeared to have lost his nerve at the weigh-in, hysterically yelling "I'm the champ! I'm ready to rumble! Tell Sonny I'm here! He ain't no champ! Round eight to prove I'm great! Bring that big ugly bear on!" Watching journalist Jerry Izenberg remarked: "He behaved like an absolute lunatic."

Come the fight, Clay was in control and dominated the opening rounds. He was simply too fast for Liston. But there was drama at the end of the fourth when Clay started having trouble with his sight and screamed: "I can't see! My eyes!" It was later suggested that coagulant used to treat Liston's cuts had got into the challenger's eyes. Clay was panicked and wanted to quit but, after cleansing them, Angelo Dundee sent him out for the fifth and implored to run and stay out of Liston's range. After a minute the stinging subsided and his sight cleared.

In round six Clay resumed control, catching his opponent time and again. Liston quit on his stool before the seventh and a new champion had been crowned.

Daily Mirror

3d. Thursday, February 27, 1964 No. 18,720

The Men with Red Faces

A TRIUMPHANT Cassius Clay screamed "Eat your words" at sports writers yesterday after winning the world heavyweight championship from Sonny Liston by a seventh round technical knock-out at Miami, Florida.

And among the red faces were those of Britain's top sports writers. For this is what they said BEFORE the fight . . .

PETER WILSON Daily Mirror
"I shall be surprised if Clay can go more than three rounds . . . a comparative greenhorn."

SAM LEITCH Sunday Mirror
"I take Liston to freeze . . . his challenger before the end of the third round."

PETER LORENZO Daily Herald
"I ride right along the champ's prediction that Clay won't be around . . . after the third round."

JIM MANNING Daily Mail
Sportswriter of the Year
"Clay . . . a rabbit if ever there was one . . . is flirting with death."

DESMOND HACKETT Daily Express
"I take Liston to win in the fifth round."

ROCKY MARCIANO Daily Sketch
"I think Sonny Liston will put him away before the fifth round. Yes, I mean knock-out."

DONALD SAUNDERS Daily Telegraph
"If Clay is still there when the fourth round begins he will have done better than I expected."

REG GUTTERIDGE Evening News
"Liston should make certain. . . . But anyway surely before the eighth round."

GEORGE WHITING Evening Standard
"I see Liston swinging an axe on a Claypigeon no later than round four."

PETER WILSON TODAY—Page 31
BIG FIGHT PICTURES—Centre Pages

CLAY'S SONNET

A poem Cassius recited before he challenged Sonny Liston for the World Heavyweight Championship

Clay comes out to meet Liston
And Liston starts to retreat
If Liston goes back any further
He'll end up in a ringside seat
Clay swings with a left
Clay swings with a right
Look at young Cassius
Carry the fight
Liston keeps backing
But there's not enough room
It's a matter of time
There, Clay lowers the boom
Now Clay swings with a right
What a beautiful swing
And the punch raises the bear
Clear out of the ring
Liston is still rising
And the ref wears a frown
For he can't start counting
Till Sonny comes down
Now Liston disappears
from view
The crowd is getting frantic
But our radar stations have
picked him up
He's somewhere over
the Atlantic
Who would have thought
When they came to the fight
That they'd witness
the launching
Of a human satellite
Yes, the crowd did not dream
When they lay down
their money
That they would see
A total eclipse of the Sonny

CHAMP
AT HOME IN BRITAIN

Now known as Muhammad Ali, he was an almost permanent presence on our shores in the heady sporting summer of 1966, defending his title against Henry Cooper and Brian London

AFTER dethroning Sonny Liston in February 1964, Cassius Clay confirmed he was now a practising Muslim, declaring: "I believe in Allah and in peace." He was a devoted follower of Elijah Muhammad and the Nation of Islam.

Within weeks he announced he wished to be known as Muhammad Ali, which he said freed him "from the identity given to my family by slavemasters".

A rematch scheduled for November 1964 was postponed three days before when Ali underwent a hernia operation. They eventually fought the following May, with Ali knocking Liston out in the first round.

After two more successful defences, one against former champion Floyd Patterson, Ali returned to Britain for a rematch with Cooper, staged this time at Arsenal's Highbury stadium.

It was the biggest fight ever staged in Britain and, having floored Ali in their first fight, there was a patriotic belief that the home hope could claim the title. Ali ended those illusions as Cooper's fragile skin forced a stoppage in the sixth.

“I figured that if I said it enough, I would convince the world that I really was the greatest

▲ **_LISTENING CLOSELY:_** _Discussing religion with a group of muslims in London, May 1966_

◀◀ **_NAME GAME:_** _The new identity is clear on the back of his gown but it was many years before 'Muhammad Ali' properly caught on_

◀ **_STARE-OUT:_** _The eyes have it as Ali and Cooper contemplate their re-match_

TUNE-UP: Rare colour images from a sparring session with Jimmy Ellis (who Ali later fought in 1971) at the TA drill hall near White City

BEWILDERING AND BLINDING SPEED

***DAILY MIRROR* chief sports writer Peter Wilson was awed by Ali's movement as he watched him spar three days before the fight with Henry Cooper.**

He wrote: 'In the ring he certainly does not behave like a normal man. Frankly, I have never seen such bewildering speed from a man anywhere near his size.

'Most of the time he concentrated on leg work, using the ring to show that it's almost impossible to hit him solidly even if you threw a handful of marbles at him.

'There was one tremendous and completely unexpected attack as Jimmy Ellis was pounded by a succession of blows which were over almost before he knew he had been hit.

'Angelo Dundee pointed out how the champion was circling always to the left, away from Cooper's best punch – the left hook which floored Ali on that memorable night nearly three years ago.'

***A FEW WORDS:* Speaking to the BBC during a walkabout in Soho**

***FACE IN THE CROWD:* Attending a meeting of the Radical Adjustment Society in north London**

***HORSE RACE:* A training run with unusual company**

DUCK: Ali takes cover as Cooper goes on the attack at Highbury

ON THE ATTACK: Cooper's bloodied face shows the scars of battle as Ali's speed and aggression again proves too much for the home hope

STROLL IN THE PARK

THE morning after Ali stopped Cooper to retain his title, the *Mirror* joined him as went for a relaxing walk.

'Unmarked, unhurt and unhurried... that was the king of boxing yesterday.

'After an early morning walk in St James's Park, Ali found his court filled with clamouring fans and well-wishers. The world heavyweight champion remained the perfect host all day – smiling, laughing and signing autographs.

'The hand-shaking, back-slapping and embracing began at his London hotel. By mid-morning, more than 30 Muslims from all parts of London had crowded into his bedroom. Ali hugged each one in turn and exclaimed: "Brothers, how good to see you."

'Ali said: "The British public have been marvellous. The last time I came here I was hollering and acting crazy, and they couldn't understand me. This time they were cheering and everything went off perfectly."'

FAMOUS FACES: Sean Connery and Diana Dors ringside for the big fight

TAKING IT EASY An elderly woman appears to be overcome by Ali's presence as he wanders through St James's Park the morning after beating Cooper

BACK IN TOWN: After just a few weeks, Ali was back in Britain to defend his title against Brian London

DOZE: A rare quiet moment amid the madness

THIS WAY: The photographers were rarely disappointed when Ali was around

FAMILIAR FACE: *Two months after fighting him, Henry Cooper shares a joke with Ali as the champion gets ready to face London*

YOUNG FAN: Mario Morin, just 12 months old, watches Ali skip

CORNER MAN: With legendary trainer Angelo Dundee, a constant presence throughout Ali's career

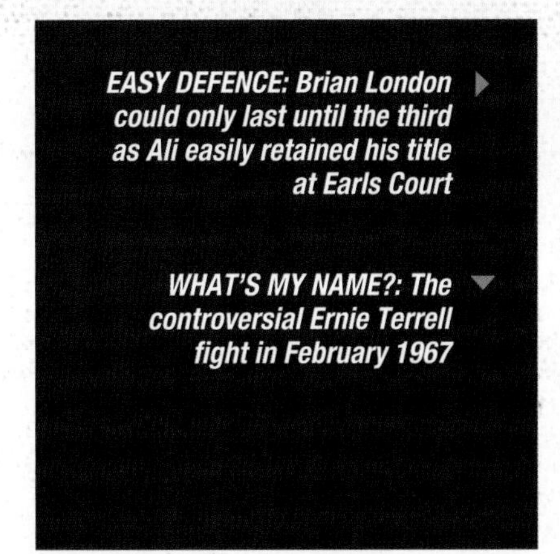

EASY DEFENCE: Brian London could only last until the third as Ali easily retained his title at Earls Court

WHAT'S MY NAME?: The controversial Ernie Terrell fight in February 1967

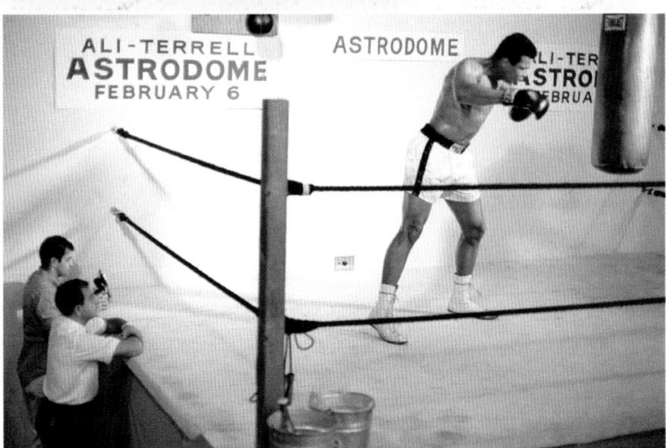

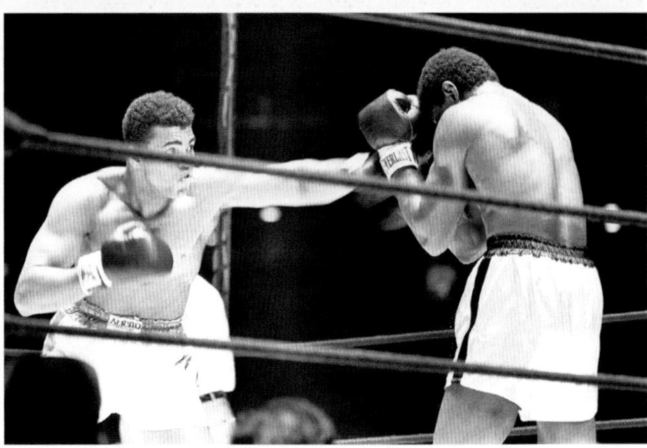

STRIPPED OF HIS TITLE AND BANNED

FROM when Cassius Clay converted to Islam and changed his name to Muhammad Ali, he polarised opinion in America. Matters came to a head early in 1967.

He defended his title in February of that year against Ernie Terrell. While giving his opponent a savage beating, he caused uproar by repeatedly spitting out: "What's my name?" to Terrell, who angered Ali by referring to him as "Clay" in the build-up to their fight.

Weeks later – after another successful defence against Zora Folley (his 29th straight victory) – he refused to be drafted into the United States Armed Forces, having famously declared: "Man, I ain't got no quarrel with them Vietcong."

The consequences of his stance were far-reaching. One hour after he refused induction, the New York State Athletic Commission suspended his boxing licence and withdrew recognition of him as champion. All other jurisdictions in the USA followed suit.

In June he was put on criminal trial and found guilty of refusing induction. He was sentenced to five years in prison. Although he didn't actually serve any time, his passport was confiscated, which prevented him boxing anywhere. Ali was effectively in exile at home and was unable to fight for over three years.

SECOND COMING

Ali was able to resume his boxing career in 1970 and within months was set for the 'fight of the century' against the new champion, Joe Frazier

AFTER three-and-a-half years when he was deprived of his right to earn a living in his chosen sport, Muhammad Ali was back in the ring and desperately wanted to reclaim the crown he felt was rightfully his.

During his absence, American public opinion had gradually turned against the ongoing Vietnam war and thus softened towards Ali, who spent a large portion of his exile explaining his social and religious views during lectures at university campuses all over the USA.

He was able to resume boxing in October 1970 when Ali's handlers realised there was no state athletic commission in Georgia so no body in that state had withdrawn his licence to fight.

The heavyweight champion was now Joe Frazier but Ali had to try to get rid of the ring-rust before challenging Frazier. First, he stopped Jerry Quarry before, six weeks later, labouring to a points decision over Oscar Bonavena in New York after a court ordered the State Athletic Commission to return his ring licence.

The stage was now set for Frazier and Ali, both unbeaten, to contest the 'fight of the century'.

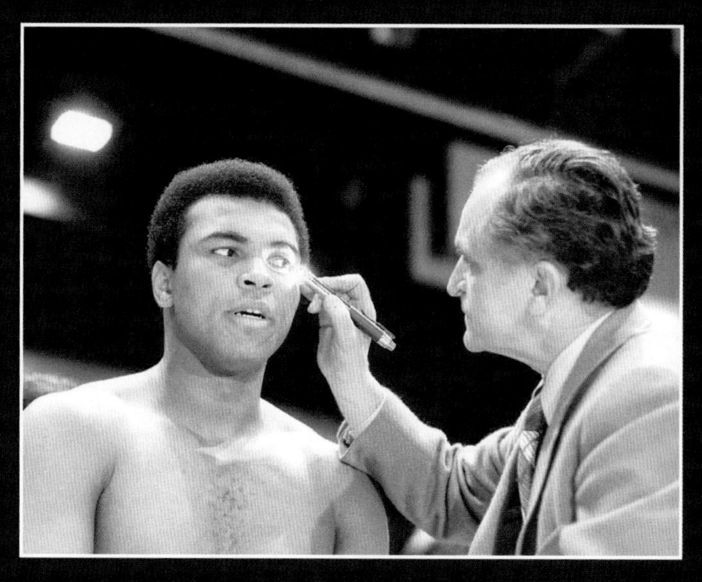

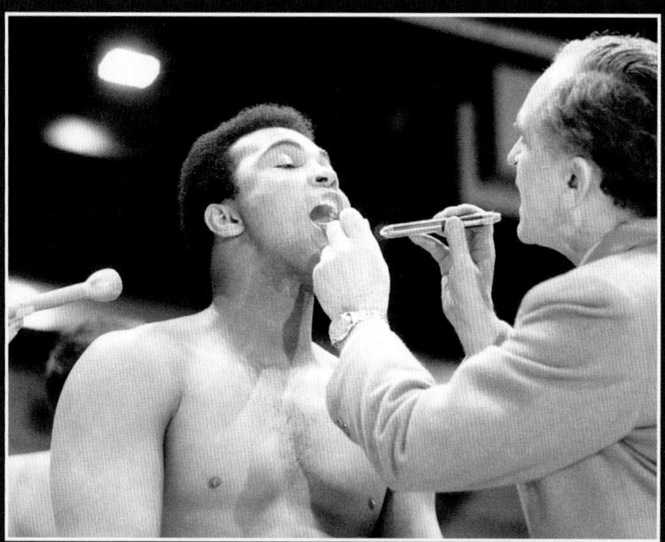

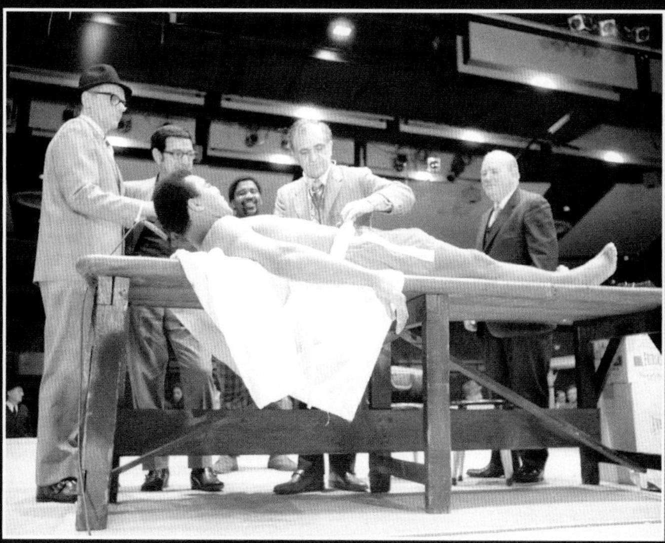

CHAMPIONS COLLIDE

IT WAS, perhaps still is, the biggest event in the history of boxing: two undefeated heavyweights fighting for the championship of the world when it was THE greatest prize in sport.

Frazier-Ali didn't require any selling but that didn't stop the challenger from trying to get inside the champion's head with insults that echoed the Sonny Liston fights: "Joe Frazier is too ugly to be champ. Joe Frazier is too dumb to be champ. The heavyweight champion should be smart and pretty like me. Ask Joe Frazier: 'How do you feel, champ?' He'll say: 'Duh, duh, duh.'"

Anyone who was anyone clamoured for a ticket. Not all succeeded. Frank Sinatra failed to secure a ringside seat but was able to get a pass to take photographs for *LIFE* magazine. Dustin Hoffman and Diana Ross weren't so lucky – they were turned away on the night.

People all over the world were gripped by the fight, debating who would prevail. It was televised in a record number of countries and 500 requests for press credentials had to be turned down.

A poem for Joe

ALI'S RYHME BEFORE THE FIRST FRAZIER FIGHT

Joe's gonna come
out smokin'
But I ain't gonna be jokin'
I'll be pickin' and pokin'
Pouring water on
his smokin'
This might shock
and amaze ya
But I'm gonna destroy
Joe Frazier

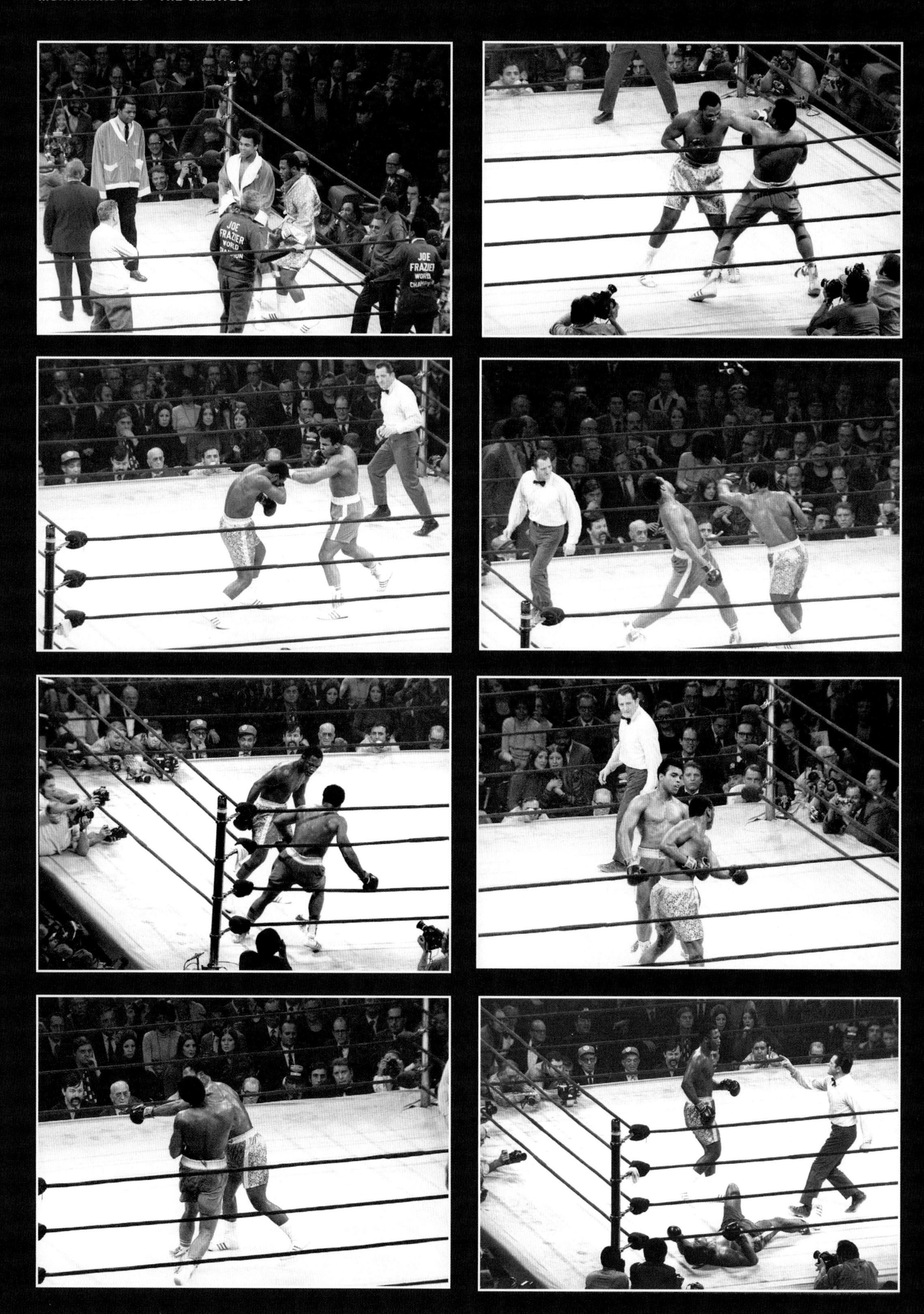
JOE
FRAZIER
WORLD
CHAMPION
JOE
FRAZIER
WORLD

INVASION: Chaos in the ring after the final bell as the NYPD desperately tried to maintain some semblance of order. Frazier won a unanimous decision

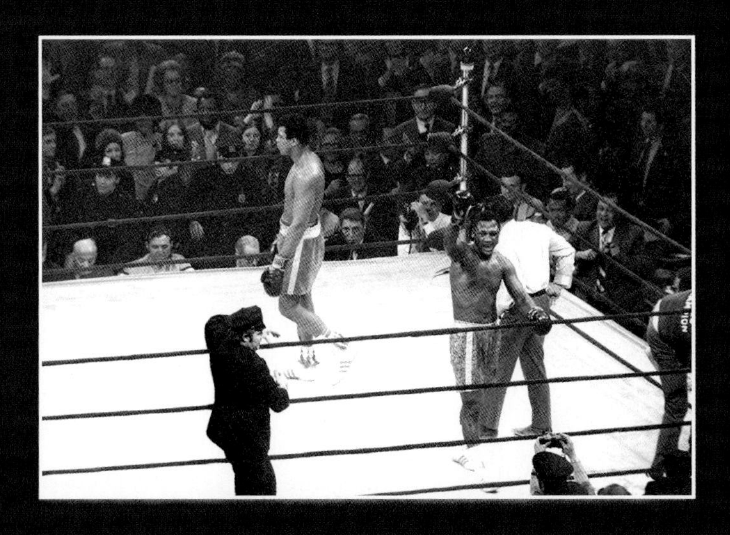

FLOORED BY FRAZIER

THERE was no dishonour for Muhammad Ali as he experienced his first professional defeat to Joe Frazier in a bout that justified the 'fight of the century' billing.

There was little to choose between them in the early exchanges but as they moved through the rounds, Frazier's power started to sap the strength from Ali, who no longer possessed the lightning speed in his legs to stay out of range.

In the 11th, Frazier caught Ali with a vicious left, which sent him reeling back into the ropes. A barrage of blows followed as the champion sought to end the contest.

The remaining rounds were dominated by Frazier and he underlined his superiority by flooring Ali with a shuddering left hook in the 15th. It was astonishing that he was able to climb off the canvas and see out the final two minutes, but there was little doubt that the points verdict would go in Frazier's favour.

The *Daily Mirror* headline referred to the 'Broken Butterfly' but Peter Wilson's report was generous towards Ali, whose face was horribly swollen afterwards.

Wilson wrote: 'In defeat, he made more friends and was so much more of a man than he had been in some of his more famous victories.'

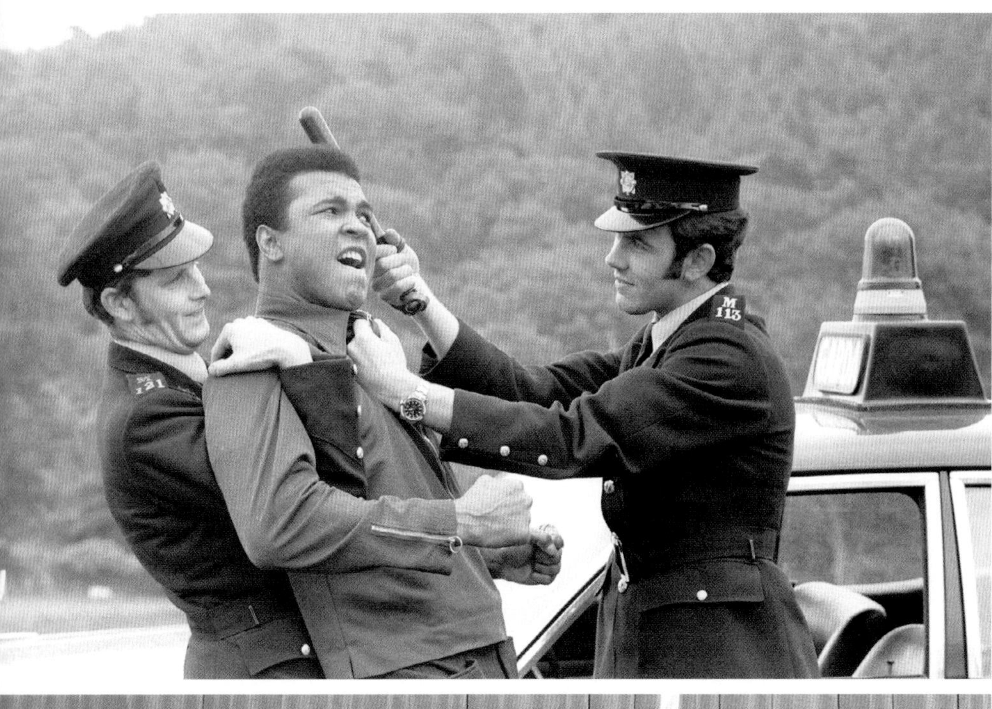

***RESTRAINED:* Former heavyweight champion Joe Louis gets between Ali and Bugner before their first fight (right) in Las Vegas, 1973**

***ARRESTING:* Playful fun with the Irish Garda before his fight with Al Lewis in Dublin, 1972**

***JOE BLOW:* Bugner took Ali the distance but lost on points**

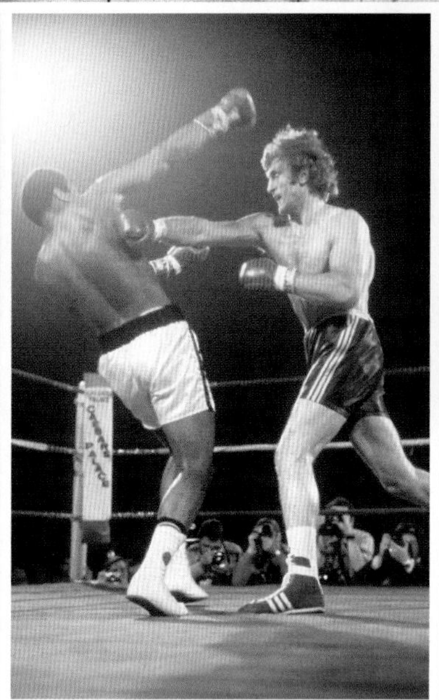

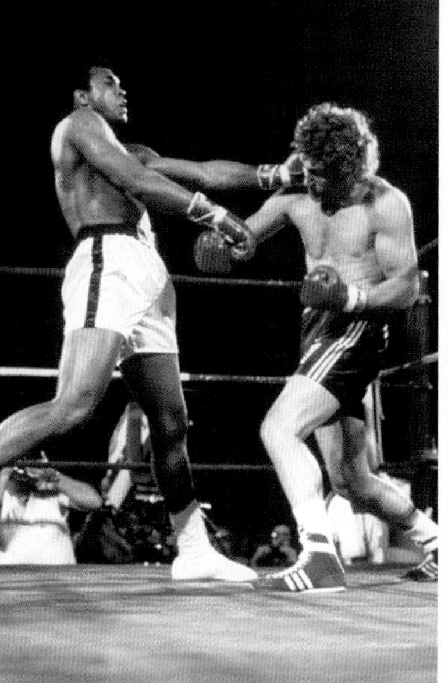

BUGNER OUTPOINTED IN VEGAS

FOR the first time since his 1966 fights against Henry Cooper and Brian London, Ali faced a British fighter when he went up against Joe Bugner on Valentine's Day, 1973.

Bugner gave a decent account of himself but his inherent caution meant he never really threatened to cause an upset and lost a 12-round decision. Ali won his 10th fight in a row since the epic with Frazier two years earlier.

Ali came into the ring wearing a bejewelled robe bearing the words 'People's Champion' – it was a gift from Elvis Presley.

A little over six weeks later, Ali entered the ring again to fight the super-fit Ken Norton in San Diego. Norton was too sharp and broke Ali's jaw in the second round, eventually edging a close points verdict over 12 rounds.

After surgery and the necessary recovery period, Ali and Norton laced up again six months later and this time another narrow decision favoured Ali, who was back on track and still chasing the world title.

ADMIRING THE VIEW: A look in the mirror while training at his camp, January 1974

ALI'S CAMP

A HOME FROM HOME

Deer Lake was the site of Ali's training camp, a sanctuary that still drew the crowds

"I COULD have gone to Miami Beach or somewhere like that to train but there'd be partyin' and women."

Ali's words above explain why, in 1972, he built his hideaway in the wilds of Pennsylvania, far away from the bright lights and temptations of big cities.

In July 1973, when the *Daily Mirror* visited, two bunkhouses slept his sparring partners, while a 3,000 square foot gymnasium, decorated with magazine covers and paintings of the man himself, was his house of pain. A luxurious trailer housed Ali, his wife, Belinda, and their children. The estate also accommodated a maid, two cooks, four horses and a great Dane called Pisces.

People travelled vast distances to find the camp where, for a dollar admission, they could watch the great man prepare for fights.

In time, as it was developed further, he grew to love the scenery and serenity of Deer Lake.

THIS WAY: The sign at the side of Route 61

CABIN FEVER

ONE hour by road from Philadelphia and two hours from New York City, Deer Lake was a five-acre site up a country road off Route 61.

It was here he trained for all his fights from 1972 until the end of his career in 1981.

When the camp first opened, large boulders were brought in to protect cars from rolling down a steep slope. The names of legendary fighters (and Angelo Dundee) were painted in giant letters on the rocks.

Ali's camp still stands today in pretty much the same condition as when he was an active fighter. After he sold it in 1997, it opened as a bed and breakfast.

FAMILY MAN: At the breakfast table with (second) wife Belinda and daughters Jamillah and Rasheda

***SANCTUARY:* Relaxing in his bedroom**

***TIMBER:* "It's not easy cutting down a tree but I tell myself that tree is [Ken] Norton and it's got to come down"**

Ali

***SPAR TREATMENT:* For just one dollar, people could watch Ali tune up for his fights at Deer Lake**

MUMMY'S BOY: Ali in the kitchen with his mum, Odessa

HOMEWORK: Watching footage of his first fight against Ken Norton, before the rematch in September 1973

LIFT OFF: Hugging a young girl while entertaining children

SWEEPER: Ali was happy to muck in with the menial tasks

***COLD BLAST:** Snow and ice on the ground on a freezing January day in Pennsylvania*

***BELL-RINGER:** The sound was familiar to Ali from his fights*

LOOK WHO'S BACK

Most people considered Ali past his prime but on an incredible African morning he shook up the world again by flooring the formidable George Foreman in the 'Rumble in the Jungle'

IT IS undoubtedly one of the most extraordinary sporting events ever staged.

The Rumble in the Jungle, in October 1974, was unlike anything seen before, as Ali challenged the unbeaten George Foreman for the heavyweight title in Kinshasa, Zaire (now known as the Democratic Republic of Congo). At that time, major international sporting events didn't tend to take place in Africa.

Ali made great play of his African ancestry to rally the locals behind him. His ploy worked and, during the build-up, "Ali, bomaye!" (Ali kill him) rang out wherever he went. The force of his personality carried the crowds, but he would be alone in the ring with a frightening opponent. Foreman had demolished Joe Frazier in three rounds to claim the world title and, in March 1974, Ken Norton suffered a similar fate, being left senseless after a brutal second-round knockout. Both Frazier and Norton had previously beaten Ali.

However, Ali, who so often defied logic, stunned the world by absorbing everything that Foreman could throw at him before knocking him out. Seven years after being stripped of his title, he was champion of the world once again.

WORKING UP A SWEAT: In training for the George Foreman fight

TWO CHAMPS: Sharing a stage with light-heavyweight John Conteh at the Royal Albert Hall

ALI'S TAUNTS

Ali was as outspoken as ever before the George Foreman fight:

"There's not a man alive to beat Muhammad Ali. Ain't no flat-footed washerwoman like George Foreman gonna whup me. I was world champion when he was in high school.

A miracle is going to be performed. When I get to Africa, we gonna rumble in the jungle.

Gonna be so fast I'm gonna hit him before God gets the news. Last night, testing my speed, I hit the light switch on and I was in bed before the room was dark.

It started raining last week. I handcuffed lightning and threw thunder in jail. I'm so mean I make medicine sick."

***READY TO RUMBLE:* Ali going through his paces at Deer Lake in January 1974**

THE PUNCH HEARD ROUND THE WORLD

BBC COMMENTATOR Harry Carpenter's disbelieving tone said it all as, when George Foreman was counted out, he exclaimed: "Oh my God, he's won the title back at 32!"

Ali's reclamation of the heavyweight title was an astonishing coronation in the early hours of an African morning that has gone down in legend, inspiring the Oscar-winning film *When We Were Kings* and Norman Mailer's reportage epic, *The Fight*.

Outside his own camp, he was given little or no chance of dethroning Foreman, who at that time was considered close to unbeatable.

After initially taking the fight to Foreman, Ali quickly adopted what became known as 'rope-a-dope' tactics, leaning back and letting big George unload all his ammunition.

As the bout reached the middle rounds, Foreman was spent and Ali exploded into action in the eighth, sending the champion to the canvas in a flurry of punches. Angelo Dundee had it right when he offered this pre-fight assessment: "He's only human; my guy ain't."

***ON THE MIC:* Commentating alongside John Motson on a bout in Britain, December 1974**

DOMINANT: Taking the fight to Joe Bugner in Malaysia

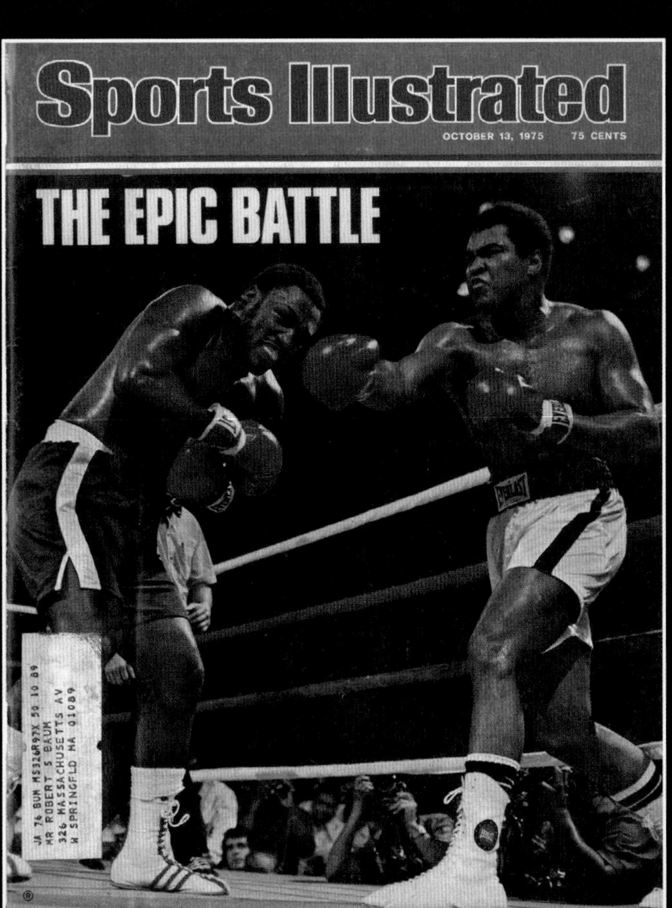

THRILLA:* *The Sports Illustrated front cover following the third and final fight between Ali and Joe Frazier

BUGNER AND THE THRILLA

ALMOST two-and-a-half years after their first meeting, Ali once again shared a ring with Britain's Joe Bugner, and this time the world title was on the line.

Bugner had won eight in a row following a points defeat to Joe Frazier but Ali was the overwhelming favourite for the daytime fight in Kuala Lumpur, Malaysia, in July 1975.

The oddsmakers were accurate in their assessment as Ali won with something to spare after 15 unspectacular rounds.

Four months later, Ali faced Joe Frazier for the third and final time, contesting the 'Thrilla in Manilla' on October 1.

It was another epic. In sweltering temperatures, Ali had Frazier on the brink in the early stages but the challenger's courage allowed him to survive and launch an offensive of his own. The two men pounded each other to the brink of collapse.

At the end of the 14th, Ali returned to his corner and instructed Angelo Dundee to cut his gloves and end the fight. At the same time, Frazier's corner man, Eddie Futch, called a halt. Both men had nothing left to give. Ali described it as the "closest thing to dyin' I know of."

***ABOVE AND ABOVE RIGHT:* Brit Richard Dunn was brave but not remotely in Ali's class. The May 1976 fight ended in the fifth**

***RIGHT AND BELOW:* Ali on the march in the lead-up to his third fight with Ken Norton, campaigning against explicit movies while denigrating his opponent. In the event, Ali was lucky to edge another close decision at New York's Yankee Stadium**

SEC. ROW SEAT
RINGSIDE $200.00
ALI vs NORTON
THE EVE. SEPT. 28 1976 8:30 P. M.
MADISON SQUARE GARDEN BOXING, INC.
PRESENTS
MUHAMMAD ALI
CHAMPION
WORLD HEAVYWEIGHT CHAMPIONSHIP
VS
KEN NORTON
CHALLENGER
15 ROUNDS
YANKEE STADIUM
SEPTEMBER 28, 1976 — 8:30 P. M.
SEC. ROW SEAT
RINGSIDE $200.00
ENTER RINGSIDE GATE - RIGHT

***ABOVE AND LEFT:* A special guest at Pele's farewell match for the New York Cosmos at Yankee Stadium in October 1977. In the image to the left, Ali shares a few words with England's World Cup-winning captain, Bobby Moore. It would be fair to describe Pele and Ali as the dominant sporting personalities of the 20th century**

***TOP LEFT:* With fellow heavyweight champions Joe Frazier, Jimmy Ellis, Joe Louis and Floyd Patterson**

***TOP RIGHT AND MIDDLE LEFT:* Baby daughter Hannah appears to identify who gets to ask the next question at a press conference**

***MIDDLE RIGHT:* Coming face to face with actor Dustin Hoffman**

The last hurrah before the FINAL BELL

After being outpointed by Leon Spinks, Ali avenged the loss to become the first three-time world heavyweight champion before his career closed with two distressing defeats

IN FEBRUARY 1978, Muhammad Ali had just turned 36 when he defended his title against the novice Leon Spinks – a 1976 Olympic gold medallist, but only seven fights into his professional career

A complacent, demotivated, out of shape Ali was outpointed by Spinks in one of the biggest upsets in boxing history.

Seven months later there was a rematch in New Orleans. This time Ali was fully prepared and he won a comfortable decision over 15 rounds, which meant he was the first man to win the heavyweight title three times.

There didn't appear to be anything left for Ali to achieve and after a few months of reflection, the man himself appeared to agree, announcing his retirement in June 1979.

Sadly, like so many boxers, he couldn't resist a comeback, agreeing to fight the unbeaten champion Larry Holmes in October 1980.

The health problems that would blight his later life were making themselves evident and Ali was a mirage of the thrilling fighter of old. Now he was just old. Trainer Angelo Dundee called a halt after 10 depressing rounds.

There was one final fight – a points loss to Trevor Berbick in the Bahamas in December 1981 – before, belatedly, Ali retired for good.

THREE TIMES A CHAMPION

IT WAS a final moment of history for a man who had illuminated the 1960s and '70s.

In front of the largest indoor boxing audience ever assembled – 63,532 – and watched by what was then the second largest American television audience in history, Ali, defying Old Father Time, was willed to victory over 15 rounds. The occasion as much as the opponent seemed to overwhelm Spinks who was 'as mesmerised and helpless as a boy trying to shovel against an avalanche' in the words of Hugh McIlvanney.

After a first round in which his timing was off, Ali established control, laying claim to the centre of the ring and picking Spinks off with jabs and combinations. Although he was penalised a round for holding, Ali was too smart for Spinks, who was shown up for what he was – a novice in his ninth professional fight. He was not helped by having too many people in his corner. Amid a din of opinion, trainer George Benton walked away, exasperated, after the sixth.

At the bell for the 15th, the decision was not in doubt. Ali was champion of the world, again.

ALL SMILES: Ali and Spinks at a pre-fight press conference before the rematch at the New Orleans Superdome in September 1978 (below)

***ROCK STAR:* Taking to the stage at a benefit variety show for former British heavyweight Joe Erskine**

***PUCKER UP:* With Joanna Lumley at an LWT gala night in June 1979**

***TOP RIGHT:* Ali loved to play magic tricks**

***MAKING A RACQUET:* Clowning around with tennis champion Bjorn Borg**

ON THE LINE: Using an early example of a mobile phone

OLD MATES: With British light-heavyweight world champion John Conteh

GUIDING LIGHT: Sharing a few words with Angelo Dundee, who was in Ali's corner for 20 years

NOTHING LEFT: Ali had no answer to the youth and power of Larry Holmes

COMING TO AN END

ALI'S final two fights were heartbreaking to witness for those who had thrilled in his majesty over the previous two decades.

In October 1980, four months shy of his 39th birthday, Ali faced former sparring partner Larry Holmes as he attempted to claim the world title for a fourth time.

It was a hopeless aspiration. Ali's reflexes had diminished appreciably. The *Daily Mirror* report described him as 'a man in the middle of a hopelessly lost cause being pounded and punished' before Angelo Dundee called a halt after the 10th round.

After one more loss, to Trevor Berbick in December 1981, the remarkable career of this extraordinary man was finally over.

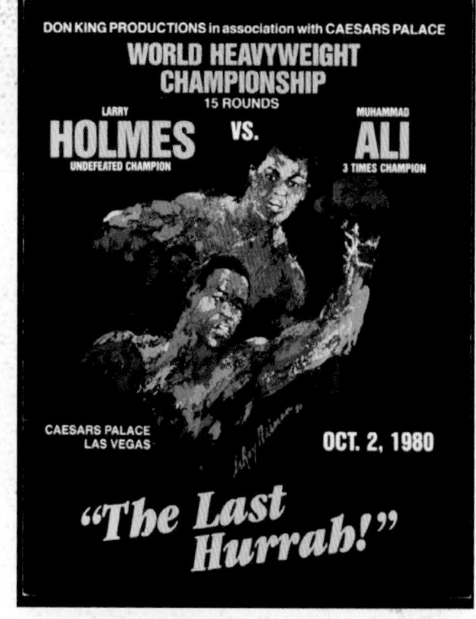

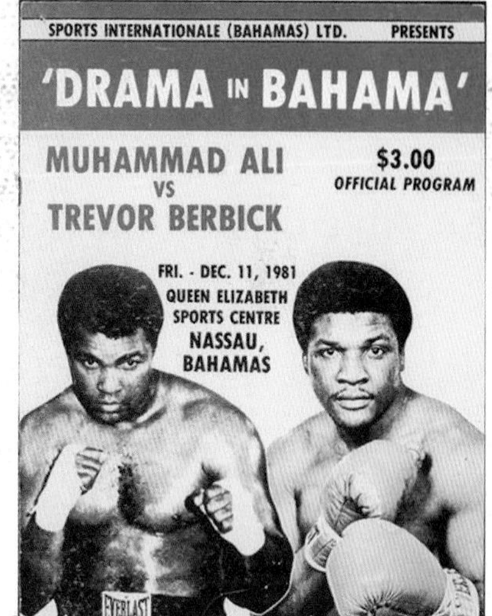

***SAYING GOODBYE:** The sign says it all as he trains for his final fight in the Bahamas*

PIED PIPER

Ali's charisma was a magnetic draw all over the world as people flocked to get near him

BEATLEMANIA was a phenomenon confined to the 1960s but Muhammad Ali had his own version that continued for 50 years and more.

There wasn't a more recognisable face in the world and, wherever he went, people followed, in their hundreds and thousands.

He was a hero to young and old, whether they had ever watched a boxing match or not.

His talent, confidence, charisma, courage, kindness, humour and presence were irresistible draws.

Although he was a divisive figure early in his career, Ali would eventually inspire adoration on an unprecedented scale. His debilitating illness diminished him physically, but he continued to illuminate our lives like no-one else.

BACKED INTO A CORNER

In October 1971, Ali came to Britain to promote Ovaltine, the malted milk drink. This is how the *Daily Mirror* reported his chaotic visit to a Tesco supermarket in Stretford, Manchester:

'A lesser fighter would have thrown in the towel long ago. But this is Muhammad Ali cornered.

Hundreds of straining, heaving fans of the former heavyweight boxing champ are pushing their admiration to the limit. He can only retreat to the unprotected 'neutral corner' between a mountain of tins and jars.

The 'bout' took place at a supermarket in Stretford. Ali was signing autographs and promoting a health drink. And more than 1,000 people turned up to cast an admiring eye on his style.

An £80 glass door was smashed. A woman fainted in the crush. The champ, worried that youngsters might be hurt, shouted: "If you don't get back, I'll have to go."

Minutes later, he did. The 'ref' – in the shape of the police and his aides – stepped in. It had all been too much. Joe Frazier was never like this.

The crowd had won a technical knockout. And the retreating champ declared: "I was really alarmed."'

LEFT-HAND PAGE, CLOCKWISE FROM TOP LEFT

FACE IN THE CROWD: *Making his way through the narrow streets of Soho, May 1963*

SIGN HERE: *In a Blackheath Youth Club, May 1966*

HANDBAGS: *Accosted by an elderly lady at Heathrow, December 1971*

THIS PAGE

TOP: *Feeling claustrophobic while promoting Ovaltine at a Tesco supermarket in 1971*

ABOVE: *Middle-aged women queue up for a kiss in 1977*

RIGHT: *Surrounded by police officers during his visit to Newcastle in 1977*

Cover star

As of May 2016, Ali has appeared on 40 Sports Illustrated covers. Only Michael Jordan, with 50, has featured more

▲▲

ON THE ROAD: *Presenting a coach on behalf of the Variety Club to Great Ormond Street Hospital, 1977*

▲

PASS THE SALT: *Tucking in on a visit to former boxer Jack Bodell's chippy in Coventry*

◄

JUB-ALI: *An open-top bus tour through Newcastle, complete with portrait of the Queen, in 1977*

SHOWMAN: Attending a film premiere in London, December 1980

MAN OF THE PEOPLE: Signing copies of an authorised biography in a WHSmith store in 1992

NEW FAN: Watching Nuneaton Borough FC during a tour of the Midlands, May 1984. He arrived in an open-top 1928 Rolls Royce and threw signed tennis balls to the crowd

AND STILL... THE GREATEST

Even past 70, Ali remained an icon loved in all corners of the world

TOP LEFT: Pictured with two of his daughters, August 1992

OVATION: An embrace from Bono, lead singer of U2, at the 1999 Brit Awards

OLD ADVERSARIES: Appearing on Wogan in 1989 alongside George Foreman and Joe Frazier

THAT LEFT HOOK: Catching up with Henry Cooper, who described Ali as "the fastest thing on two legs I've ever seen"

RIGHT: With Lennox Lewis and Harry Carpenter, who commentated on so many of Ali's fights

AN ELDER STATESMAN

LIFE was not kind to Ali after his boxing career finished, as Parkinson's disease slowly but surely diminished his physical capabilities.

The man himself made few concessions to his condition, continuing to tour the globe and promote good causes despite the all-too-evident ravages caused by the progressive, degenerative disease.

His slurred speech and slow, shuffling gait were apparent to all from the early 1980s. It was at the 1996 Atlanta Olympic Games' opening ceremony when the deterioration in his health was starkly exposed, as he courageously struggled to light the Olympic flame while his left hand shook uncontrollably. Sixteen years later, when he featured in the opening ceremony for the London Games, wife Lonnie had to support him when he stood up.

Ever since the onset of his illness, Ali never sought any sympathy or expressed any bitterness at his failing health. He simply accepted it and continued with his work, maintaining a gruelling schedule that belied his age and infirmity.

Throughout it all, he brought joy and excitement to all corners of the world, which will always remember the unique personality of one Muhammad Ali.

THE LIGHT STILL SHINES BRIGHTLY

IN DECEMBER 1999, two days after he shared a stage with Ali at the BBC Sports Personality of the Year awards, *Mirror* boxing columnist Barry McGuigan wrote a passionate article about his hero after a large television audience were shocked by Ali's frailty when he accepted the main award:

'Muhammad Ali is an emotive topic. People see him shuffling along flat-footed. They hear his words uttered slowly and watch in horror as his hands shake uncontrollably. They look back at what he was and feel tremendous pity. And when they do, they insult the greatest sportsman of this or any other country.

Ali is a proud man and wants no-one to feel sorry for himself. Furthermore he would not change anything about his career. Given the opportunity he would do the same again – engage in great gladiatorial conflicts with Frazier, Foreman and Norton, endure the thousands of miles of roadwork, the pain and agony of life in the ring.

It defined him as much as he defined the sport. It is seductive to lay the blame for his ills at boxing's door. There is a link between dementia pugilistica and straightforward dementia but no expert could, hand on heart, say with any certainty that Ali's condition resulted directly from boxing rather than his genetic inheritance.

The man himself accepts his fate with good grace and gets on with it. The same spirit that drove him in his magnificent career is evident today. People with Parkinson's don't fly around the world, crossing endless time zones, because they just can't cope. Ali does. If he lay down and gave in it would consume him quickly. He never was a quitter and he is not about to start now.

To sit on the same bench as him in the BBC studio on Sunday made me feel so proud. To be recognised by him is to be honoured. When I looked into his eyes I knew that behind the inscrutable mask, the same inventive, witty intelligent human being knew exactly what was going on around him.

The information goes in, but does not come out as he would like. I'm told it is an immense frustration for Ali that he cannot express himself as he did. In that, his eyes have become a key tool. The light has never left them.

For me, he does not need to speak. He has said all that needs to be said. That did not stop him aiming a gentle aside in my direction, which threw me just as surely as a left hook. As I began my reply to John Inverdale's question about the century's greatest fighters, Ali listened to my eulogy about Evander Holyfield and Lennon Lewis before looking at me and whispering "but I'm the greatest."

I was just about to say the same thing. No-one heard it and it put me totally off my stride. I thought then that there was nothing wrong with his brain. God bless Muhammad Ali.'

OPPOSITE PAGE:
Holding his trophy after Ali was voted BBC Sports Personality of the Century in December 1999. Lennox Lewis, who had just become heavyweight champion, won the sports personality award for that year

TOP: Posing with David Beckham at the BBC awards

ABOVE: Taking in the acclaim after being awarded a gold medal at the 1996 Olympics in Atlanta. It was a replacement for the one he won in Rome in 1960 but later threw in a river after he was refused service at a 'whites only' restaurant

LEFT: A handshake with European captain Nick Faldo at the 2008 Ryder Cup, which was staged in Ali's home city of Louisville

POIGNANT: A final meeting with Henry Cooper in August 2009. Cooper died less than two years later

IRISH WELCOME: Visiting Ennis in County Clare, the birthplace of his grandfather

ICON: Taking part in the 2012 London Olympic Games opening ceremony

ALI AT 70

MIRROR writer Brian Reade, who interviewed Ali in 2001, paid a personal tribute on his 70th birthday in January 2011:

'I can still feel the intensity of the adrenalin rush as Muhammad Ali emerged from a car and stumbled towards me at his Michigan ranch. I can still see the living legend, despite suffering a horrible disease that crushes lesser men, attempting to show me his boxing skills in the gym. His right hand was shaking violently as he tried to bring the wild muscle tremors under control and slowly will it towards the big bag.

In 2001 there were roughly 6.2 billion people on this earth. But only one who I wanted to meet so badly I'd have swum the Atlantic with an old bed tied to my legs.

Muhammad Ali may by then have been a frail, sick man 35 years past his peak, but it felt like I was being treated to the most potent sporting image of all time: the poetic pugilist in action, floating like a butterfly, stinging like a bee, your hands can't hit what your eyes can't see. And I felt so humbled. Because when I was a kid in the '60s and '70s, he was the king of the world. The man whose fights in the early hours of the morning on the other side of the globe would be the first thing half of Britain wanted to know about when it woke up.

When writer Norman Mailer called him "the very spirit of the 20th century" he was right. That hundred years threw up many greats: Einstein, Churchill, Presley, Lennon, Eisenhower, Pele, Mother Teresa, Superman... but next to Ali they wilt. They wouldn't hit like him, dance like him, look like him, rap like him, crack a one-liner like him, take a stand like him, come back like him. They didn't possess his magic.

When I spent that day with him in 2001, I found my emotions alternating between awe and pity. He would fall asleep, take minutes to raise a cup to his mouth and go into a trance. But I could still find the giant within the wilting shell.'

KING OF THE RING:
Ali – the way we will always remember him

THE VIEW FROM THE TOP OF THE WORLD: London, July 1966, looking down from what was then known as the GPO Tower